Feel, Heal, and Enjoy

13TH & JOAN

For permission requests, write to the publisher, addressed "Attention: Permissions Coordinator," 205 N. Michigan Avenue, Suite #810, Chicago, IL 60601. 13th & Joan books may be purchased for educational, business or sales promotional use. For information, please email the Sales Department at sales@13thandjoan.com.

Printed in the U. S. A.
First Printing, May 2022.
Library of Congress Cataloging-in-Publication Data has been applied for.

ISBN: 978-1-953156-76-1

Feel, Heal, and Enjoy

By Lovelee Lundy

Contents

"Aspire to Inspire before you Expire!"

— *EUGENE BELL JR.*

I dedicate this book to my intelligent son Cairo; may it always be a reminder to follow your dreams. You inspire me every day. I love you more than anything in the world and beyond. You deserve me at my very best and I'm working every day to give you the better version of myself than I was the day before. I want you to remember that nothing is impossible for God. Watching you grow is an honor. You amaze me and make me proud every day.

Feel, Heal, and Enjoy!

I have never taken a poetry class or even read a how-to book on poetry.

In all honesty, I had never even read any of my poetry in public until July of 2021. It was for my 30th birthday and like this book, it was a present to myself.

I was nervous to say the least. I decided for my birthday celebration that I wanted to do something different and that's when I noticed that a local lounge in Portland was hosting an open mic on my birthday. So, I said why not, if I am going to do this, I'm going all the way. I got dressed up and I was with two of my besties, Brionna and Jackie. I added my name to the sign-up sheet and waited to be called. My entire body shook with nervousness. I was encouraged to drink to take the edge off. With each sip my hands steadied themselves and before I knew it, they called my name. Emotions swelled as I froze with fear again, tears rolling down my cheeks. The moment had come.

What if they hate my poem? What if there is nothing but silence at the end? What if I… what if I… what if I…

I took a deep breath and began. The more I read the more confident I felt, as if the power of my words flowed through my body. I was no longer crying. I felt so empowered. I completed my poem and as the realization of what I had just accomplished settled in, I was greeted with applause, cheers, and hugs, not just from my friends, but from so many surrounding strangers. All of them wanted to show their support. I had never in my life felt so much validation. Throughout the night so many people came to me and expressed how I made them feel as if I were speaking directly to them. And although I love and accept support from any and everyone, the crowd was predominately Black, and I think that validated more for me than just my poem.

Feel, Heal, and Enjoy is special to me because it's my vulnerability in written form. It's a poetic display of both shared second-hand emotions as well as my own emotion, captured in a moment of time. We all feel emotions, some of us more deeply than others. I believe that I have a heightened empathic awareness and I soak in emotional energy. At times that energy weighs me down like I'm carrying emotional baggage. This energy can stem from an event that is happening directly to me and indirectly around me. Poetry is how I release that energy. I can take something so powerful and make it soft and beautiful.

When I'm overcome by a strong emotion, I feel impelled to release it. My poetry is that release in a finished form. Many, if not all, of these poems have been written anywhere from 30 minutes to an hour. I don't focus on what I'm trying to say but more so how I want it to feel, how I want the reader and or listener to feel.

My earliest memory of writing poetry was when I was about 12 years old. Mostly silly things about school and boy crushes, but when my world changed after I was raped at the age of 14, I changed … and so did my poetry. It became an *escape*. A coping mechanism if you will. *Feel, Heal, and Enjoy* is my emotional life story. My poems are of love, loss, encouragement, fear, injustice, life, and managing it all. The title is a play on the phrase, "the devil comes to steal, kill, and destroy," so this book is to help feel, heal, and enjoy. This is not an advice book, it's just my personal opinion based on my personal experiences, and I know it's not going to be appealing to everybody and that's okay.

I've been fighting my entire life. Even before birth the odds were stacked high, but my God stood higher. The day was Tuesday July 23, 1991 when I arrived. The first of many times coming back to this world. I was 3 months premature. Weighting in at one pound six ounces. I died! But God knew I had so much to offer this world. I was fragile but I was a fighter, I still am. The full story of my birth is another story for another time, but I fought so hard to be here, to live, and when you fight that hard, you don't take life for granted. Writing is my destiny and I believe this is me fulfilling my purpose.

I pray this book finds the person that needs it. I pray for peace, love, and blessings for everyone that reads it as well as the ones that don't. I want to share with you this expression of me in hopes that you can find comfort in our common emotions - knowing that although you feel what you're feeling, you aren't feeling it alone. If I could help one person, just one, then everything leading me up to this moment was worth it. So, thank you. I pray this helps you like it helped me and I hope you can feel the emotion and power of each poem just as I intended.

Poetry

(10/27/2015)

Sometimes I'm feeling philosophical
And other times I'm getting murdered by my obstacles

The mistakes I've made I'm trying to bury deep
But I keep getting slapped in my face by defeat
The same horrors keep happening to me
Like a nightmare on repeat, better yet Elm Street

I'm stuck in a conundrum that I cannot run from
I got life backwards like dragons and dungeons
Ima old soul trapped in the body of a younin'
My mind is wondering
Should I keep pushing forward or go back to where I come
    from?

This is why I love poetry
It poisons me
Slow drip, like an IV
So, I can show off the poise in me
I am the definition of rhythm and artistry
If you look deep enough, you'll see the art in me

Every click of the pen is my heartbeat

And on every inch of the paper my heart leaks
If I lost this gift, it would make my heart weak
I'm ok now, but wait until I hit my peak

This is my life, if I failed to mention
I make words come alive, you can see my composition
I strive for precision
I revise my revision
So, I consider the mirror my only competition

I could walk on air and still manage to stumble
Could have an easy touch down and still manage to
        fumble
Could be made of stone and still manage to crumble
So, after every blessing I give thanks to God, and He keeps
        me humble

Family

"You don't choose your family. They are
God's gift to you, as you are to them."

— *DESMOND TUTU*

Mom

05/27/2016

In your womb you planted a seed
Your love helped water me
Your wisdom was my guiding light
You watched me bloom day and night
You were the first touch I ever felt
And you taught me how to play the cards I was dealt
Even when I wanted to do it by myself
You waited patiently until I needed your help
I don't know your full story and I can't begin to try
But when I think about your love for me, I can't help but to cry
You must have super strength because you carry so many
        things
Like love in your heart
And the pain life brings

I know life's no easy trial,
But we walk the road together hand in hand with a smile,

I will forever love you, you own my heart
I could never pay you in full, I wouldn't even know where
        to start
I'm well into adulthood but I still wish upon a star
I hope I'm granted the privilege to become at least half the
        women you are

Living in Peace

11/18/2020

I could easily harbor hate for a man I don't know
And believe me it's not easy to let it go

I know that it wasn't doing me any favors, yeah, it's true
But I used to repeat to myself as a kid how I hated you
Stood on my own two feet, thank God that I made it
    through

Now that you are gone
All I can say is so long
No love lost and no harm done
Inadvertently there are so many things you taught me
Like how not to accept disrespect
And how to keep others from hurting me

But I still have demons lurking and disturbing me
Now that you're dead and gone I have to learn to live in peace
Reluctantly I had to come to grips with my reality
Daddy's little girl is something I'll never be
Having you walk me down the aisle is something I will
    never see
You were blind to the fact that you incapacitated me

I'm sorry for the cards you were dealt
And the life you were living
But for my own peace of mind
All is forgiven

Farewell

09/25/2013

With a tear I smile, with a smile I tear
Only selfish of me to wish you were still here.
Every moment a lesson of love
Every breath is a borrowed blessing from above.
I asked God to hold us in our time of sorrow
And help condition our hearts today and tomorrow.
Your work was finished.
Your job was done.
So, God whispered to you, "come home my son."
In obedience, you obeyed
Although many of us wish you would have stayed.
You're in a better place since you've moved on
Your health won't fade you
Your pain is gone
So, I say farewell and bid you adieu
And in my prayers each night, I'll say hello to you

Dear Cairo,

03/19/2019

I believe in your dreams
And I believe in your heart
I believe you can achieve anything you start
I believe you are smart

Never say you can't because I believe you can
You will grow to be an exceptionally intelligent man
It's all in God's plan
It's all in the works

I believe you were destined for greatness prior to birth
At times life will hurt
But there are lessons in pain
And even if the world changes
I pray your heart stays the same

Full of love and full of hope
Never full of hate because you will regret it
A good heart is worth gold so be sure to protect it

I believe in you

You are priceless, not just in terms of wealth
So most importantly
BELIEVE IN YOURSELF!

My Child

02/17/2019

Don't stress
You are blessed,
Keep your head up
Apply pressure
And remember, never let up
No matter how many times you fall you've got to get up.
I'll always be by your side so don't give up.
A lot of your friends will be foes trying to deceit you,
Never give someone a second chance to mistreat you.
Beauty is internal, your external is just a feature.
God gives lessons, during the test there is always silence
        from the teacher.
Love yourself
Love your soul
Love your mind

Know it's necessary to be alone sometimes
I know it will be scary to hold your own sometimes

But you my child will be just fine
I foresee greatness in your future
Love in your heart
Knowledge is power

And know there is a difference in being wise and being
        smart
And when someone shows you who they are, believe them
And if you get bad vibes from anyone it's okay to walk
        away without a reason

12

Never make anyone feel less than
Never stand for anyone trying to make you feel less than

Greet the janitor as if he was the CEO
And wear your confidence like an overcoat
Put God first and everything else will follow
Your pride and ego will be like the truth,
They are hard pills to swallow

Be humble
Don't mumble, speak clear
Don't let others speak for you or through your ear

Know your worth because it will take you far
When you know yourself, others cannot tell you who you
    are.

Rise above and be great
Love trumps hate
Freedom trumps failure
Faith trumps fate

Believe in yourself, for I believe in you
And with God by your side, there is nothing you can't do

Dear Anthony:

09/20/2014

I see your pain

But I don't know if our fears are the same or not
To be clear, do you shed tears or not?

Does your pain affect you the way it affects me?
If I reached out, would you extend your reach or just let
    me be?

Or turn me away?
I will love you in the past and the future the same as I love
    you today
We share blood, we had a bond
Dear friend, where have you gone?

Our paths didn't happen to cross
You are my brother
Tell me, are you lost?

Have you strayed away from who you were to become?
Have you given up and said you're done?
Seems like you've lost track of what matters, you see
Even if I don't to you, you still matter to me

Have you forgotten about your family?

Say it isn't so
Say that we live in your heart and you'll never let us go
Say that you miss us as much as we miss you

Say you haven't replaced us, say it isn't true

I pray for you brother
With tears in my eyes
Hellos are what I want to say instead of goodbyes

I just want to hug you and give you a kiss
Know that you are loved
Sincerely, your baby sis

Happy Father's Day

06/08/2016

On this day I celebrate you
Because in absence of our father
You helped see me through
A girl needs her father
This I know to be true
But I thank God with every waking breath
I was blessed with a brother like you

I don't really believe in luck or chance, just fate
Your presence was right on time, not too early not too late

The saying "mama's baby, daddy's maybe?"
I guess it still holds true, my mother taught me how to be
    a lady
But I learned what a man was, solely by watching you

I don't know if you know the extent of your impact
But over the years my growth and success,
I have you to thank for part of that
I just want you to know you've impacted my life in such a
    major way
So, I celebrate you Fred, Happy Father's Day!

If Heaven Had a Phone

10/19/2014

If heaven had a phone, I'd be the first in line
To tell you I can't live without you,
And you'd respond, "you'll be just fine."

The hold music I'd imagine would be the sound when
angels sing
I'd dial your number, smile, and hold my breath with
every ring

I'd tell you everything I never got the chance to say
I would appreciate the small things like if you asked me
about my day

I'd call you every chance I got, don't get me wrong
But it's heaven, so every now and then I'm sure I'd get a
busy tone

Number one on speed dial
Every time you'd call, I'd smile

We'd never get enough time and how do you properly say,
"so long?"

I scream to heaven each night

Because heaven doesn't have phones

No call waiting, 3-way calling or even morse code

So, I'm stuck with distant memories and your love that I'll
always hold

I guess I don't need a phone because I have prayers. Yes, I
do!
So, if God is not too busy, maybe he could get my message
to you

My Super Ability

09/06/2014

The picture is painted
The blessings are not done
The smoke has cleared
The war was won

But my battle still goes on
With that, you give me space
As if I don't see the looks and
glares of ignorance upon your face

The whispers behind my back as if you're afraid of me
But the only thing you should fear is your own self *pity*

Many people don't know my story
At times it seems surreal
And although my behavior may be different
You should know, I still feel

If you look down on me something within yourself is weak
But even when I am silent, my autism speaks!

My Black Reality:

"Hate, it has caused a lot of problems in the world but has not solved one yet."

— *MAYA ANGELOU.*

A Voice

11/23/2016

How can words make a difference
If no one will listen?
Too caught up in their own afflictions
To even bare witness
To see that the key to humanity could be within me
Or the man on the corner trying to sell his CD
They rather stand in a shallow sea of hypocrisy
I get too deep,
it's no wonder why they can't follow me
They choke on the truth
So, their unable to swallow me
I could be a cliché on the runway, and they still couldn't
    model me.
How can I be heard if I'm drowned out by nonsense?
Lately everyone has an opinion, but they all lack content
Claim to be conscience but overlooking monsters
Standing in plain sight and they are still unresponsive
Being passive aggressive hoping the aggression is passing
Acknowledging the issue, but still not reacting
We're lacking, back tracking, what is really happening?
I'm fighting for a chance, well writing for a chance, to get
    in on the action
I'm no politician
I'm not here for free healthcare and rising tuition
Just here for Black welfare and to inspire ambition
Working for better days, not just wishing
I'm not asking for too much
I'm just asking that you listen

Stand Corrected

12/04/2016

This guy comes to me and says, *"You are beautiful to be dark skinned!"*

My reply?
"Wait! Are you implying that a beauty standard is based upon complexion?
Because when I look at my reflection
Trust and believe I'm not stressing
I wear my dark skin as a badge of honor, a blessing!"

This guy looks at me and says, *"Why are you mad? That's a compliment."*

My reply….
"I am confident that is no compliment
And I am second guessing your consciousness
Because the consequence for such incompetence is the revocation of your common sense"
I had to explain how I once was refused a date, not based on sight
But type, because my skin color wasn't light
Yet I didn't fuss or fight
Just wished him a goodnight
Because one of us was wrong,
I knew I was right
And arguing would have been an unnecessary plight
He wasn't too bright
Besides, arguing with a fool is like feeding a parasite.

Then he tells me *"you're blowing it out of proportion"*

I told him *"tell that to the girl who is bleaching her skin*
Trying to fit in
Changing her exterior
To feel prettier within".

He said, *"she's just confused, you know"*.

I looked at him with the side eye
And replied *"no, you're delusional*
This isn't new you know
But I shouldn't expect you to know
So many brothers like you refuse to know
You pick and choose the truth
So, you don't think it's unusual
That your viewpoint has been misconstrued'

He looked me dead in my eyes and said
"Beauty is in the eyes of the beholder"
The look on his face implied he'd never made a statement
    more bolder

I said, *"that's true*
But look back at our history
Complexion had been used as a weapon to divide us consistently
And if you have a type that's your prerogative
But don't base that type off of a brain washed cognitive"

With sincerity he apologized and said, *"I had never thought*
    of it from that perspective."

I told him *"don't be sorry, just stand corrected"*

A Black Man's Nightmare

07/06/2016

Everyday is a struggle
For a Black brother
But on that exact day
It wasn't quite like any other,
Yet similar to another
Because once again a son is being buried by his mother.
We need to repaint the picture
Ensure its painted clear
Sad that this world is tainted with so much hatred and fear.
It's been said before
But I guess you can't hear
Man, this right here
Is a Black man's nightmare.

You had him on the ground, bound, and surrounded
And I'm sure not guilty was how the verdict was founded.
I'm sure for you it was easy to pull the trigger
Because in the back of your mind he was just another
    nigga.
This is more than an epidemic, this is a gimmick.
He is today's hot topic
Then tomorrow it's back to business
Until the next body drops without a word or witness.
Please tell me how this is right?
I'm counting more funerals than celebrations of life.
Too many Black men are in jail,

They're incarcerated at a rate almost five times more great
     than whites
I guess that's why there aren't many daddies around to
     kiss the Black baby's goodnight.
They are going to pick us off until there is no more left
Didn't you know being Black is punishable by death?
They will scream gun even if it's all clear
A crooked cop is a Black man's nightmare.

The streets are flooded with their blood
Minds roam free in a closed cage
Enraged, afraid, and portrayed as dangerous
Funny because the cops' guns are aimed at us.
Death is possibly a dispatch away
And they wonder why we are afraid.
Our screams are being silenced by our plea
It's like being lynched from our very own tree.
This is not a Black man's nightmare
It's his reality.

Expectation

06/11/2016

I've been disrespected, rejected, and neglected, and yet
    expected to excel
Oh wait, I misspoke, what I meant to say was I'm expected
    to fail.
I've exceeded every obstacle and yet they repeat it until I
    accept defeat
But what they don't know is with each leap I master my
    technique.
See I know what they are planning,
So even if I stumble, I make sure to stick my landing.
I am determined to be the last man standing
And because of that they can't stand me

They refuse to revere us
So, they choose to fear us

They saw something that most of us can't see
They are not physically afraid of us
They are petrified of the potential threat we could be.

I've been disrespected, rejected, neglected, and yet
    expected to forget
Oh wait, I misspoke, what I meant to say was I'm expected
    to submit.
They will extend their hospitality to a certain degree
And they want me to be happy
After all, "you could do a lot worse"
Like doing a life sentence behind bars
Or taking a stroll in a hearse.

They speak with such certainty
Certainly they can see why we steer clear of uncertainty.
It's them who needs us
Yet we have been conditioned not to bite the hand that
    "freed" us
I guarantee we would be just fine if they ever decided to
    leave us.

I've been disrespected, rejected, neglected, and yet
    expected to answer to nigga
Oh wait, they misspoke, what they meant to say was
    Negus
We are kings and queens and yet some still don't believe
    us.
We have been reprimanded and offended for the color of
    our skin
But our skin glistens and compliments the royalty within
The different array of beauty only we can create
No longer shall we debate and separate each shade
When we share the same fate
Even in darkness the spotlight is bright enough for us all
    to be great
So, keep your head up so your crown will forever remain
    straight

And next time you feel disrespected, rejected, or neglected,
    expect it but don't you dare accept it.

Injustice

09/03/2014

There are some people who would like to swerve and forget
But we're being gunned down by the ones who swore to
    serve and protect

If you are a good cop, then you should expose the bad
If snitching isn't your style, then you should let go of your
    badge

Stand with the people in the streets
Because your badge is the only thing keeping you from
    being me

The truth is hard to swallow like a mouth full of spit
A disgusting taste is stuck under your tongue, making you
    want to vomit
You have a nauseating feeling in the pit of your stomach
I am a writer, some would call me a scribe
And I must do my best to keep my history alive

No I didn't boycott, sit-in, or ever removed a noose
But the chains of racism aren't broken
They have merely been let loose

A mother is in grief
We are weak
We are not dead to our history,
We have only been asleep
Man killing man

We are not human yet mere beast on a safari
On the timeline of freedom please tell me where are we?
Mentally enslaved, materialistically engaged
Our actions are like diamonds
Worthless until someone comes along and gives them
     value - now they have purpose.

United we have more power than the stars
But justice isn't just locking someone behind bars

Its teaching morality
Testing mentality

Hoping that the results surpass their vindictive ways
We cannot correct the past, but we can correlate better days

It's not just Black history
It's your history too
It doesn't matter if you're white, black, brown, yellow, or
     blue
Injustice here is injustice everywhere
Whether you're being discriminated by your color, height,
     size, sexual orientation, belief, disability, age, gender,
     or hair

We idolize status
But have minimal compassionate apparatus
We need a leader,
Tell me who is next?
Or are you going to "yes massa" your way through life
     because they sign your checks?

And when I say "they" it's not specific to a race
It's an individual's choice to propagate hate
It's not a genetic trait

It's only spread if your mind isn't vigorously constructed
    to know the truth
So they target the youth
If you view a fight and refuse to help, you are just as
    wrong for speculating
So if you see discrimination and stand down, you're not
    racist
But you are just as guilty as the ones discriminating
We have no right to use, abuse, discriminate, hate, or
    mistreat

Oxygen fills our lungs
And gravity still grounds our feet
We are unique in personality,
but we are the same in humanity.
Show compassion,
be a littler kinder.
We aren't that different; this is just a simple reminder.

Our Power

05/24/2016

I had to take a step back
Quick to brag about what I had
But wouldn't admit to what I lacked,
I was misguided by stereotypes
And instead of believing in myself
I believed the hype,
I spent too many nights hoping,
Never realizing the key to my chains was in a book yet to
    be opened,
Instead of fixing what was broken
I was on the path of destruction
Even when I seemed to have it all, I had nothing
If I didn't know who I was, how could I do this?
I looked in the mirror and realized I was clueless
I was never behaving in a cultural manner
Only the way I was programmed to
I asked myself a question,
Who programmed you?
And just what was that program meant to do?

For starters it was designed for me to be uncomfortable in
    the skin I'm in
To question the loyalty of our men
To never think I could be greater than I am
To divide us so we could never stand on our own
To never again have peace in our homes
They thought destroying our crowns
Meant we would never again take a seat on our thrones
But they were wrong

They didn't count on the fact that that their program could
    be hacked
We were robbed of our history but it's time to take it back
It's time to act
I'm so glad I took a step back
I can now share the knowledge I have
And build where I lack
Kill the propaganda of stereotypical Blacks
Not only do I believe in me, I believe in my community,
Unity
Not spending another second hoping or wishing
If the door to opportunity is closed, then we're going to
    kick it in

I looked in the mirror and realized that self-love is the fuel
    that feeds me
I have faith in the man that will successfully lead me
The possibility is infinite to how great we could be
Let's start by taking back our communities
Build our families, our unity, and communities' piece by
    piece with whatever we can find
So, we not only have peace in our homes
We'll also have peace of mind
Let's teach our children so they can grow into prominent
    kings and queens
It's time to show the world what our power really means

Masterpiece

05/26/2016

I've stumbled upon a masterpiece
Shortly after I mastered peace
How fortunate I must be.
I have so many places to start
For example, his mind is like a work of art
And his heart is calling my name
His touch makes me want to erupt
It's no wonder why I fell so abrupt
I welcome this change
His kiss is timeless
Making me forget what time it is
I swear time stands still

What I found is priceless
How dare you try to price this
This rare artifact has been analyzed, classified, and identi-
    fied as real
It was not meant for all to see
just me
he is such a historic piece
hidden in the lies of history
covered in the shame of wrongdoing
I see his worth, that why it's him I'm pursuing
I will protect him
Respect him
Dissect him
I need to know every color of his fiber
Because one day I will reflect him
This masterpiece has me in awe

What I see as unique
Others see as a flaw
I opened my eyes and here you are
Glad to know I'm not dreaming
I refused to share you with the world
Because many choose not to see what I'm seeing
Even in night
Man, what a sight
They could never dim your light
You were stolen
But found your way to me again
My masterpiece
My Beautiful Black man!

Living in Fear

03/23/2021

My anxiety is at an all-time high
Running me ragged to the point that I can't go for a run
    outside
Go to the corner store
Or have a broken taillight
Because an everyday action could cost me my life
I sit down and think back,
There was never a day we were safe being Black
being berated, hated, and constantly attacked
Living in fear
This isn't fiction, all facts
They stormed the capital, man look at them niggas
Crossed state lines with a rifle and pulled the trigger
And of course, he walked away scott free
I can't even walk ten feet and not have the cops stop me
Feels like I have a low survival rate
Feels like the clock is ticking down on an unjust date
Thought I could be safe if I stayed in the house, just don't
    leave
But that means nothing because they could just Breonna
    Taylor me
We're walking with a target on our shoulders
And they call it a chip
Blood stains and this pain is hard to forget
I mean no disrespect but saying their name isn't going to
    change it
I mean no disrespect because I honor them all
And I'd scream the loudest if it would cause this rigged
    system to fall

I can't speak for the community
I can only speak for myself
I'm tired of living in fear, trying to protect myself,
More so I'm trying to protect my son
Cause I'll be damned if you take him by cell or by gun,
When it comes to help, I don't know who to trust, so I
    don't know who to ask,
And for Cairo, I'ma keep fighting this war until I breathe
    my last!

Dangerous

09/08/2016

I'm young Black and dangerous
My education is infamous
It's a heinous crime
Of those trying to endanger my mind
Painting a picture of negativity
To clog my mind with stupidity
But they won't stop until they see lividity
But I will show them vitality
I'ma be hot to the touch like the devil himself swallowed
    me
They have brainwashed my king and he can't recognize
    me
Taken my ring and robes and left me exposed
Now a bigger butt and money are my only goals?
I have taken the coils and dregs and replaced them with
    hair from someone else's head
I used to have standards
Now I'm just standing
I used to have morals
Now I'm just mortal
I am a recreation
I'ma disgrace

At least back in the day they fought with grace
But now we fight with guns, locks, and mase
Can't even practice proper mannerism without someone
    "Hatin"
This is a genocide we're creating

When a white man kills a Black man, we take to the streets
    and riot
But when Trey kills Jay, we're quiet?
Since when was murder not double sided
I guess it's just double standards
Many questions get unanswered
It's not all who will wear those shoes
But it's a few, oh yes, it's a few

Some of yall think you're real
And you are
You are real two faced
But you don't care because you get wasted
Popping bottles for everyday occasions
You're hood rich
And as long as you have that mentality, you'll forever be
    grounded
Drug addicts, drug dealers and violence have you
    surrounded
How can you feel free struggling to breathe?
Suffocating underneath an equal opportunity derived sea
You are mentally locked
And today's hip-hop has you blocked
Thinking that's what it's like to be Black in America
Chains and hysteria

This topic will forever be debated
If you want to be dangerous.
To be a real threat you must be educated
And I don't just mean diplomas and degrees
I'm talking about self-preservation
Putting an end to the genocides of our generations
Stop lacking potential and patience
Explore your greatness
Stop allowing others to define you
Take the time to go find you

And in time
You'll find truth
There is more to life than what you call home
More to life than your comfort zone
You have the potential to be a phenomenal being
But first you must remove the obstacles that are preventing
    you from truly seeing
Life, truth, and all the possibilities.

America

03/10/2015

America the beautiful
America the great!
Land of the free!
Well, that's up for debate
When the going gets tough
We turn to our faith
Right to bear arms in all fifty states
President is Black
I call ObamaNation
Some people don't like that
They call it an abomination
One thing we do right
we fight for this nation
Load up those army trucks
And have our soldiers stationed
We have planted trees of pride without even knowing
Corrupted by the greed so the seeds not growing
Speaking of corrupt, time to change the subject
I'm not trying to become enemy of the pubic

America the futile
America's ambition
Kids are the future
But they are messing up the vision
Unity is sold.
Truth is told within our division
We don't talk it out
We stack our ammunition
We put band aids on Black amputees

But go marshal law over white kids with skinned knees
Someone please

Tell me

How do we have overpopulated jail cells
But claim to be free?
We're told never forget 9/11
But never speak on slavery
Crazy me
I forgot I'm not supposed to show bravery
I'm supposed to be grateful for what America gave to me
But who am I? I just make up three fifths of humanity.
And if I speak too loudly, they will try to silence me
But still I'll rise from the earth in which I've came
Sadden by my ancestors' struggle
But empowered by their pain
Even in death I will remain
Because I was told the pen is mightier than the sword
And as a reminder I briefly look back when I'm walking
    forward
So even in death, the truth I'll be walking towards it
America the beautiful
America the great
Welcome to America, the land stained by blood and cursed
    by hate

War

07/07/2016

If joy is coming in the morning
Then its war is tonight
Tossing and turning it's no wonder, I can't sleep at night
If the fee is right
Them boys in blue will be seeing white
And that may be someone's mentality type
I'm not here to tell you that it's wrong or right
I'm just trying to get you not to believe the hype
Because the truth is, no amount of money can equate a life

Another truth is we were never equal

Always on the outside looking in
they just reversed the peephole
Some, not all, are pure evil
Trying to eliminate diverse people
You are on social media debating faith
Yet another brother is staring down a barrel of hate
And you're mad because he is not Black enough?
Or her skin's too light?

But in their eyes, we're all niggas because we aren't white
But Ima stand for what is right while you sit and type
And hopefully I can inspire you to log out and fight
Let's agree to disagree but unanimously understand that it
    is sad
And the death of a Black man is worth more than a hashtag
Stop waiting for someone else to clean this mess

Grab a rag

Don't these streets being flooded with our brother and
    sisters blood make you mad?
Violence isn't the answer
Peace isn't the question
We are repeating the same cycle
We have forever been stuck in

Unapologetically Black

07/29/2016

I won't apologize for my large thighs
And milk chocolate skin
My almond shaped eyes
Nor my structured chin

I won't apologize for my distinctive nose
And large distinguished hair
My professional clothes
Nor my "Thug" wear

I won't apologize for my big succulent lips
And the community in which I was raised
My childbearing hips
Nor my road to success being unpaved

I won't apologize for the way some of my sisters and
      brothers behave
And the food that I may or may not eat
My physiological damage from my ancestors being enslaved
Nor my history being secrete

I won't apologize for wanting more than you're willing
      to give
And the opportunities being locked
My willingness to live
Nor kicking down the door rather than giving a knock

I am sorry for not focusing on what I had rather than
      what I lacked
But I'll never be sorry for being unapologetically Black.

Empowerment:

"There's nothing more beautiful than a
smile that has struggled through tears."

— *NICKI MINAJ*

Living with Monsters

07/03/2021

Calmness, stillness, and peace of mind
Seems to evade me each and every time

Feels like I'm running but my feet won't hit the ground
Looks like I'm screaming but I never make a sound
Could I be dreaming?

This can't be my reality!
Hell of a nightmare, monsters living inside of me
Depression and second guessing, it's my anxiety
Strips me bare and paralyzes me
Head under water, I can barely breathe
I don't recognize myself,
Only fragmented pieces of me
Only an empty shell casing of the person I used to be
Only the shadows are left to accurately identify me
I can't stay in this dark place
This prison wasn't designed for me
So, I grasp at the light, the hope, and the possibility.

I have scars and bruises, the battle hasn't been kind
But as difficult as it has been,
I'm choosing me each and every time

So, I'm not waiting for the monsters to consume me
I am breaking free
I'm sure calmness, stillness, and peace of mind are on the
    other side waiting for me

Women

10/25/2015

She has a face that inspires nations.
I never met her, but I admire her patience.
She doesn't know but I pray for her daily.
I know so little, but I think she's amazing,
She is something you wouldn't believe.

Go ahead make a liar out of me
Doubt her and watch her achieve
And all she asks for is love, protection, and loyalty

Her body has been stolen
She is broken
But will still crack a smile even with her eyes shut … swollen

Queen by birth
Not knowing her worth,
Hidden talents
Her words are few,
But if you hurt her, she'll have some words for you.
She is strong even in the depths of her despair
And if you need her, she'll be there
All she requires is that you care.

She has birthed and built a nation
She has power but feels forsaken
For granted she has been taken.

She has power
She has grace

Carried the burdens of the world on her back with a smile
    on her face.
She feeds the world from her breast
Gives her best
Lost rest
And consistently endures stress
To know her is to love her and if you know her you are
    blessed.
Every *she* is unique
From her curves to the words that she speaks.
Even if she's beat till she drops to her knees,
She'll never fail to rise to her feet
And that is what makes all women phenomenal

Future

04/14/2017

I can't wait until my name carries some weight
And the next lesson learned is not the outcome of a
    mistake
I won't have to stress about bills or my next payday
And I'm blessed to do as I please each daybreak
I can't warn myself about years in the past
But I can be sure my kid won't have to travel my path
Have you had to face something in your life so bad,
That you're tapped out of tears, so you have no choice but
    to laugh?

The night I was robbed of my innocence
I cried on the floor thinking, this is it
That incident was no coincidence
And at 14 years old I didn't do anything for that karma to
    exist
And for four years I never spoke one word of it
Like so many others I kept my head down and just tried to
    keep up
Looking back, my silence was fear based
I was too afraid to speak up
Carrying around baggage twice my weight, and people
    wonder why numbers were so high for the child sui-
    cide rate
We're living in a world full of real life evil
Sick minded people
And they blend in so well you'll never know they are
    deceitful

Cheers to my strength
I overcame every obstacle
Turning impossible
To its possible
I am making success mandatory rather than letting it
    remain optional
30% physical and 70% logical

Most people think they can make do with one's wealth
Piss poor mentality because they have no clue how to be
    true to oneself
Ears at attention like a fictitious elf
Some will read you like a book and put you back on the
    shelf

Forget a predetermined disposition
Talk to yourself if no one else is willing to listen
Yes, people are going to look at you crazy from a distance
But you're doing it for yourself
Not for their attention
And you will be brainstorming
While they are reminiscing
You'll be complete
While they are searching for what is missing.
Beware of fake love
And thieves plotting on your ambition
Because they will rather see you dead
Than in a powerful position.
But if you learn how to dodge
You can sabotage their mission.
Ask God for vision
And you can walk into your future with pristine precision
But keep in mind the path you take is ultimately your
    decision

One Day

01/26/2021

I've got to get back to me
I've got to feel free
I've got to do the things that make me happy

I've got to stop that doubting
I've been in my mind screaming and shouting
I've got to realign my energy

I've got to start learning
My financial earnings are double, NO, TRIPLING!!!
I speak it into thee

I'm speaking patience
I'm meditating
I'm letting go of negativity

I'm going to stick it out
I'm worth it, without a doubt
Even now I'm proud of me

I'm changing what I choose to see
I'm becoming the best version of me
Thank God, The Stars, and The Moon

Someday I'll look back on this
Someday I'll say, "I did it sis!"
Someday will be one day real soon

She

09/25/2014

She is a daughter
A sister
A friend
She is a goal achiever
A dream chaser
A believer
One day she may be a mother
She is life
She gives life
She's the rays in the sunshine
The protector of unicorns
She is talented
She is our history
Our future
She is trusting
She needs protection
Her personality is as unique as her fingerprint
She is intelligent
She is the beginning of something amazing
With a smile that never ends
She is special
She is underestimated
She is powerful
She is royalty
She is a girl
She is beautiful
And most importantly,
SHE IS ENOUGH!

Survivor

10/23/2015

She is stunning
But she couldn't be sure
Her past had her feeling insecure
She was rich in love, but not in wealth
She loved everyone except herself.

One too many heart breaks
One too many lies
One too many "I'm sorry"
One to many cries

She was in a relationship she had to fix
Or he would be judged by 12
While she would be carried by 6
She got out but was still in captivity
Mentally enslaved by her own insecurities

Her mind made up
She stayed prayed up
She found love she never knew existed
Then life got twisted
And she believed God fixed it.

She got happily married
Had a kid of her own
She said *as long as I live, my faith will be strong*
Things got better
Her worry was lifted
But the devil moves quick

The roles were shifted

Went in for a mammogram
Came out with negativity
Seems like cancer is her new enemy
The devil tried to break her
But he couldn't shake her
With every treatment she gave, thanks to her maker
She spoke to women whose stories were like hers
Encouraged them to continue to be fighters
She never asked once, *God why me?*
2 years later she was cancer free

Too many lives lost each year
I pray for the fighters, the survivors, and the ones no longer here
I wish I could tell you everything will be okay
Know you are strong, and you are loved, just take it day by day

Be Yourself

09/15/2018

You must feel, heal, and enjoy love
Because the enemy will steal, kill, and destroy ya

The only battle lost is the battle not fought
Wealth doesn't come from money but rather from what
    you've been taught

So quit daydreaming girl,
Quit reminiscing
Learn to live, love, and laugh, but also learn to listen

That negativity you speak could be why your blessings are
    missing
Speak health, wealth, and prosperity rather than sneak
    dissing

Learn to control your emotions and control yourself
Because if they control you, so does everybody else

Life is hard! Yes,
But the world owes you nothin'
If you're going through hell keep going, end of discussion

Love yourself first
Know your worth
You are enough
Keep your head up and please don't give up
You came into this world alone, unless you are a twin
And you are going to leave alone in the end.

So, make sure you're comfortable in your own skin.
They could never be the real you girl
They only pretend!

Human

12/29/2016

They are trying to redefine masculinity
Making the love from one man to another an obscenity
Creating confusion and enemies
All before the tender age of three.

"Wipe those tears, real men don't cry."

Is that the right reply to an injured child looking for
        comfort?
But all he receives is condemnation?
Leaving him to grow up and believe that only a woman
        can bare softer traits such as patience
And despite all the stress he faces
He lies daily and tells himself he will be okay.

He is defying his nature
Modifying his behavior

But what happens when he reaches his peak?
And uncontrollably unleashes all that he has buried deep?
He weeps.

He is not weak
He is not to be reprimanded for being a human being
And in all the things I've seen, the last thing we need is
        another stereotype

Crying is NOT a sign of weakness
It could be a mental reminder of a time you were hurting

He cries

He bleeds

He sleeps

He eats

He is human

Fear for Freedom

03/09/2015

Imprisoned mentally
I thought I could never be free
I was bounded by fear that surrounded me
Negatively affecting
Misdirecting me

I valued more of what others thought of me than what I
    thought of myself
I knew I had worth, but I couldn't comprehend my wealth
I was shelved
Like a toy never again to be played with
But this Pinocchio must make real changes
I had to learn discipline
And never again pretend
Like I don't matter.
Not only am I the frosting on the cake, I am also the rich
    sweet batter
My body is mine
My heart is mine
My crown is mine
And I will reign until the end of my time

Because my Father God is a king you see
Doors have unlocked because I am the key.
And although I've done wrong
I can't deny the right in me
The right to be free
I have made the bed that I've laid in
But choose not to stay in

I got up to make a trade in

Fear, for Freedom

Next Stop: Freedom

09/18/2014

As she walks through the door, she feels so much pain
She has her baggage in tow as she boards the evening train

It only has nonstop destinations to pain and fear
At times she asks herself, why am I here?

Her daunting thoughts were ever so hurtful
She'd rather walk a thousand miles than continue to allow
    her pain to hurtle

But she sat on that train and tolerated the ride
Disregarding how she felt, she'd run and hide

Then finally she had to make a choice to do or die
Do what she loves or die on the inside

She steps off the train, she chooses to live and thrive
She has a long road ahead, but she feels like she's arrived

She was not weak, only tied down by discouragement
Now that she is free, she doesn't question where her worry
    went

Her baggage contains emotions and damage she couldn't
    contain
She left the baggage onboard and promised herself never
    again to board that train

She has come so far but she isn't done yet

For now, she watches from that station as the train perishes into the sunset

New Me

09/24/2018

I was drowning
Water surrounding me
From the top of my head to the souls of my feet
I was in too deep.

But my skin was dry
Why?

Because I was suffering from a mental attack
It hit so quick there was no time to react.

All I could do was cry
Internally I wanted to die
At 14 years old I wanted to try,

Not actually understanding the weight of that decision
Next thing I knew my depression went into remission

Only to rear its ugly head again 12 years too late
But now I love everything that I used to hate

I am stronger now than when I was at 14 years young
Smart enough to realize I have power in my tongue

I'm winning although I haven't officially won
I have so far to go and I know I've just begun

But the audacity of this disease harassing me
Don't sit well with me. So I choose to breathe.

When I saw change, I didn't run, I embraced it
Faced it, chased it like my life depends on it
Put my own spin on it
Because change is not necessarily good or bad
It's scary but necessary

For growth, for hope, for a new perspective
I had to just accept it

And the 14-year-old me is happy I did
I'm telling myself I am one proud kid!

Free Yourself

05/09/2021

This is the time to free your inner self
But you believe all the lies and recede in yourself
Saying you're not good enough, Man you're cheating
    yourself
You're just too afraid to believe in yourself
But there are far worse things than to be by yourself
Just give it a try and you'll see for yourself
Stop sleeping on you
Stop living a lie and start living your truth
Sounds like to me you've got some work to do
But the only person stopping you is you.
Stop being your enemy and your own biggest critic
You know what I'm talking about because we've all did it
Stop with the self-harm or the self-hate
Stop trying to sabotage what you will make great
It's time to stop getting in your own way
Tripping yourself up every single day
Why are you afraid of your own potential?
Do you not realize that you are quintessential?
Your glow up could be off the charts, so exponential.
But confidence is the key
Just know that you are essential
You are beautiful
Yet beauty doesn't define you
You are beautiful *and*...
So many other titles to add
Don't hide, take pride in what defines you
You are incomparable, don't let anyone box you in
Self-love and abundance should lock you in

Set goals, pray, and meditate
All the baggage that you carry is to alleviate
Make peace with the past so you can heal
Don't self-medicate
It's time to feel
Sit down with your emotions, sit down with your thoughts
Have an honest conversation, a real heart to heart
It's time to be free from the heartache and free from the
     pain
Just smile and know your life will never be the same

Love:

"Love sometimes means letting go of
something that isn't right for you. It's
important to walk away from toxic people
and things going on in your life. Love
gives you strength and courage."

– BY LUCILLE CLIFTON

Amnesia

02/06/2009

I wish that I could hit my head and be hospitalized
To be diagnosed with amnesia to forget all the lies

A is for the attitude that I always had
M is for the many times I ended my day mad
N is for you never being satisfied with just me
E is for my everlasting love that will burn through eternity
S is for my sanity that I came close to losing
I is for my integrity that you continue abusing
A is for amnesia a simple memory loss

And to forget you, I can forget all the pain you caused

You took my smile
You took my pride
You took everything when you lied

You put hatred in my heart and left me heated
All when you "mistakenly" cheated
I wish to hit my head and be hospitalized
To be diagnosed with amnesia to forget all the tears I cried

Craving for Love

03/01/2010

I'm insane to be craving for love
Sent from heaven straight above
Why is love what I seek?
Maybe love is what I must defeat

Love hurts
But what's new?
I can't say the words *I love you too*
Searching for love in this big world
I lost love when I was no longer daddy's little girl

I bet those two years were the best
But he left me, so love for daddy has been laid to rest
Then my first love hurt me the most
couldn't get what he wanted so he went ghost

Now I replace love with hate
Ever since the day I was raped
I close my eyes and I pray
Knowing that I will be okay

Craving for love but all I find is lust
But finding love is a must
I'll find it one day you will see
If I truly want to find love, I must start with me

I Hate You

04/10/2010

If love is hate and hate is love, then I hate your guts
Because of your charming personality that really drives me
     nuts.
I love the heartache you gave me
I love the pain you caused
The tears you made me cry
And the memories that are now lost.
I hate the way you look at me every time you talk
I love that we're not together
And I love your new girlfriend
I love that this is not a fairytale and we had to end.
There is a lot of things I hate,
Yeah, you know that's true
But the thing I hate the most is,
I hate you.
This poem is confusing because I'm confused, can't you
     see?
Because I hate you so much
Look at what hating you has done to me

I am confused!

Til Death

08/23/2016

Is it only when I'm buried deep
That you will speak of your love for me?
You said you'd bring me flowers but tell me, when?
I guess when my body is being lowered into the ground,
    only then?
Will you ever shed a tear?
After my casket is closed and I am no longer here?
Is that when you will tell the world that you loved me so?
That love, that I never saw because you would never show
Is it then?
That you wouldn't be able to resist me
Wanting to kiss me
Even if it's a kiss goodbye
If I asked you the truth
I'd bet my life, you'd lie
And now that I'm dead to you I guess I won that bet
And you'll show up to my funeral without an ounce of
    respect
Dearly departed we are here in memory of a bro-
    ken-hearted girl
Who believed that love was all that was needed in the
    world.
And as the eulogy fades
And everyone walks away
Will you remember my love?

Toxic

10/13/2016

Why is it that when I extend my reach,
The bullet in me goes another inch deep?
Does that mean I'm choosing you over me?
Am I allowing you to kill me and I just can't, see?
I am so focused on saving your life
That I am distracted from the fact that I'm about to die.
Does that make me a hero or just plain stupid?
Because the truth is, once you're safe you will walk away
And I will lie there bleeding wondering if I'll be okay
Wondering if someone will save me like I saved you
But
they
never
do
So, I either must save my own life or lay there and die
The pain is excruciating, emotionally that is
The physical I'm sure I can live with
But the thought of what you did was enough to kill me
So, I erased it from my memory.
Why is it that I feel I must save the world?
Yet I can't save myself?
Now I look at what I gave the world
And realize I have nothing left
Because I was taken for granted
And you were taking advantage
You claim not to understand it
You walked away from the impact without a scratch
Yet I'm bruised up and bandaged
Emotionally damaged

All I ever wanted was my love reciprocated
But you never participated
And now you precipitated
All the aggravation, frustration, hesitation
Now you are making faces and telling me I'm replaceable.
Are you mad because I put you on a hiatus?
Good girls finish last, man y'all really do hate us
Claimed that you loved me but that was all that you were
    claiming
Once, I was willing to take a bullet for you, now I'm doing
    the aiming

Flatline

07/02/2015

You are on the operating room table
Your heartbeat is unstable
I can't make miracles
Only a masterpiece
And I'm patiently trying to master peace
I want to create a work of art
so I'll operate on your heart
and stitch it with the colors of love
I've been told what's beautiful
but I want to see your beautiful
your beautiful soul

I have embodied my emotions
Feelings deep and wide as the ocean
Only to realize
I am paralyzed
From the top of my heart
To the point of it
Lately I see no point of it
I have been injected with too much pain
Rejected for doing the same
Although he hurt me first
He claims I hurt him worst because I never returned
How could I when I'm still searching for me?
Whenever I catch a glimpse, I run from myself because I
    hate what I see

And the next guy,
I feel sorry for the next guy

I am broken and in need of repair
And I know it's not fair
And before I could take away his final breath
I left
Unable to bare the pain I might one day cause
My excuse was that I was changing
And he didn't know me
And who would have thought years down the road he
would be comparing me to the old me?
The unlikely contender
The only man who could successfully befriend her
What if I make you flatline?
And that blame will be all mine
And I can't give you 100 CCs to revive you
I've lost my heart
I can't let you die too

What Is Love?

09/26/2014

I only miss you when I'm breathing
I only love you when my heart is beating
I only think of you
Every minute of every hour
In the car or in the shower, putting on clothes or watering
flowers

You have become my addiction
Yet you are a contradiction
So I sit down on the bed
Every thought racing through my head
As I stare at your picture
You have a beautiful smile
But ugly lies
The face of an angel
with deceitful eyes
you hold me in your right hand when my confidence lacks
and in your left, you hold the knife that pierces my heart
from the back

when we were together I felt alone
you've pushed me out and on my own
if this is love then I don't want to be in love with you
because you'll never change, it's true
you have a big heart but its frozen
and I can't walk away out of fear I've been chosen

What's the definition of love?
Is it measured by time?

Is it in my heart or my mind?
Emotions are a dangerous game
Am I dumb or clinically insane
For loving you
The way I do?

Damaged Goods

11/19/2016

I am broken at my base
And therefore, I've been replaced,
Put upon the clearance shelf
Just to take up space,
No longer can I sit in the window
Oh, how I miss the customers I used to greet
Each and every one, everyone and each,
I have been rejected, only to turn the other cheek
I was once the shopkeeper's prized possession
And now he doesn't even look at me
I've been marked down
And he didn't even think twice
I've been set on the shelf, being overlooked and judged
People wondering if I'm worth my price
I did nothing wrong
I didn't commit a crime
I am a victim of life
As well as a victim of time
I am broken as of now and that is understood
But with love, time, and care I'll be better than ever
And therefore, I am nobody's damaged goods

Self-Love:

"There is no shame in Black beauty."

— LUPITA NYONG'O

Forgiving You for Me

11/26/2021

I forgive you
And everybody else too
If you've ever put me down
Or took me through.
All is forgiven

I even had to forgive myself
Now I am able to live for myself

Forgiveness looks good on me
It has taken me to heights
I never thought I'd see

Basking in my own ambience of peace
Like I'm being kissed by the sun ever so softly
I forgive you to free myself
From the pain, anger, resentment, sadness
The madness
That was trying to consume me
That doom and gloom that drew me into your toxicity
I have broken free.

I hope one day you can forgive yourself too
But as for me and my peace, I forgive you!

Feel, Heal, and Enjoy

11/24/2021

Don't give up on yourself
You got to look up to yourself
You got to remember not to forget you
Heal baby girl
Please forgive you
You are enough
You got this
You are incredible
Your greatness is inevitable.
Your love is infectious
It runs deeper than the ocean
God's blessings
Are already set in motion.
You just have to take a step towards effort.
I know you're chained down by depression
But you have to save yourself.
Have you forgave yourself?
I mean, sat in the rawness of your emotions and from an
    honest POV replayed yourself?
Do you love who you see?
If not, you need to remake yourself.
Recreate yourself into a version you don't need to heal
    from.
A better life for yourself, brick by brick you can build one.
It's not L'Oréal, it's hard work and you're worth it.
This is what you've worked so hard for,
you deserve it.
You don't have to wait
You can run up and take it

Make it your own, this opportunity shouldn't be wasted.
Take 3 deep breaths and let them flow with ease.
Thank the pain of the past and let it go with ease.
The devil came in to steal, kill, and destroy
But I'm here to help you feel, heal, and enjoy.

So, In Love

11/24/2021

I fell in love last night
She really blew me away
The way she saw through me
She really knew me
And she loved me anyway
Yes, I am coming out in my own way
I'm ignoring your judgments and your comments
She told me to be brave.

And she quotes, "in order for you to insult me I must first
    value your opinion."
She is so smart she got my head spinning.
To throw quotes on me,
I love how deep and open she can be…
and with me, what an honor...
honestly the honor is on me
That she can feel so comfortably

She sets goals and achieves them
Her loyalty is to the ones on her side, she would never
    leave them.
She'll give till her last,
She is honest about her past
She only been in love once, and she also committed
    treason
She broke a few hearts without rhyme or reason.
But she's growing each and every day
and I'm honored to be on this journey is all I can say.
Because she is me, or at least the woman I am today.

I'm recommitting to myself in such a loving and nurturing
   way.

Believing in myself and having my own back.
And celebrating my beauty. Every crease, curve, and crack.
Celebrating my Black! I'm celebrating like, "Yes, I'm
   back!!!!!"
Celebrating like, "I did that!"
Round of applause
Like clap, clap, clap!!!!
To know yourself is to love yourself
And I am in love with every inch of me
Right or wrong
I'm loving the person I'm meant to be

Loving me

11/24/2021

I have found a love so deep
That I listen to love songs and think of me
I have never felt so free
As the warmth of self-love courses through my body
I am the love that I seek,
My own security,
My happiness and peace,
I've started retraining my thoughts
So I can regain what I lost,
Or rather put away for safe keeps
And put away the mask of depression
In response to how this world had damaged me.
I have stitched and bandaged me
And now I must heal, and the warmth of self-love melts
      the final seal
I feel complete
And I apologize as well as forgive myself for not doing
      better by me
But I am a "better now me"
And "it's a better day me"
And "it's going to be okay me"
I have to put down the mask and face myself again
And in the battle of Me VS Myself,
Love will always win

The Skin I'm In

04/11/2021

Melanated,
Priceless,
My brown skin is golden.
Out of all the fine silver,
My brown skin was chosen.
I wear it like a badge of honor
It makes me feel emboldened.
It's not a target
It's not a trend
It's like fine silk
It's so comfortable to be in.
My skin is kissed by the sun
My skin is hugged by the night
It tells the historical story of struggle, pain, and sacrifice.
My skin glistens like glitter sprayed upon my face
Although *some* may not,
My skin is something I love to embrace.
To not love my skin (scoffs) would truly be tragic
Because it's one of the many things that defines my Black
    girl magic

Being Me

09/06/2014

I trust too much
I don't speak up
And at times I don't fit in
I am not perfect
But I am worth it
And I'm one heck of a friend.
I'm just different and a little strange
But would you rather have someone who is just the same?
Like everybody else?
Someone who couldn't think for herself?
Is that who you want me to be?
Because that's not me
I am no rebel
And I am nobody's fool
I'm average at best
I don't think I'm super cool.
I'm just a plain Jane
I think my own way
I agree to disagree
Charge up my crystals
And liberate my inner chi.
I will annihilate anyone with a statistical ideology of me
I don't have competitors,
I am my own competition
Each day I try to outdo my last, that's my greatest
        conviction.
Even in death I will stand tall for all to see
And I will never apologize for being me

My Standards

09/10/2016

I am flawless with my bare face and natural hair
Unique
Another could never compare
We are discrete
No two women are the same
We should coalesce, not compete.
Washed away the insecurities caked upon my face like
        makeup
Stripped away all negativity as I seductively twirl around
        the pole of freedom
Laugh as I demolish the very box that society tried to con-
        fine me in
I refuse to be seen and not heard
I am considered sensitive, emotional, and weak
Yet try to knock me on my back and I'll land on my feet
Because lord knows I can't stop
I am society's rock
That has kept that wobbly leg stable.
And yet I'm still asked what I can bring to that table?
My heart has been shattered but it still beats
My hands are strong enough to hold together my family
And gentle enough to wipe tears from your face and put
        you at ease
My lips strong enough to form a loving kiss
Smart enough to know when to unleash the beast formally
        known as my tongue
Because the words I speak have brought grown men to
        their knees
I bare life

I endure sleepless nights
I carry an overloaded heart
I can be a sister, mother, aunt, friend, or wife
I am on the clock 24/7 because there are no breaks in life
I am forever on duty
So, know this, I am my own standard of beauty

Rise Above

01/30/2019

They fell in love with my flowers
They fell in love with my fruits
They fell in love with my beauty
But only I've watered and nurtured my roots

I was once a weeping willow
Now I'm more like a Japanese cherry blossom
I used to think of myself as awful
Now I know I'm so awesome

I am strong and resilient
And I tell a story like no other
I may be in a row of many
But I am unlike any other

I provide shade not throw
Peace of mind and nourishment, I grow it
I am beautiful and I know it
I am confident and I show it

My beautiful coils resembling leaves
Stacked high atop my crown swaying in the breeze
You may look at me as one in the same, to you I'm just a
    tree
But as I grow and thrive there is some much more to me

I've been planted with purpose
Watered with self-love
Captured the hearts of many

And no matter if I'm cut down I'll still rise above

Isn't it ironic that my ancestors used to hang from these
    trees?
There is beauty in every ugly thing you see
So look at me and tell me all the beautiful things that you
    get to see
My ugly truth is I used to need others to validate me

Not anymore
So, negativity,
I will just abrogate thee
Mentally I rose,
Now I'm finally free

Upgrade Her

09/29/2019

I am not her
And she is not me
I am everything that she couldn't be
I'm grounded, like the roots of a tree
I am so free
The universe speaks to me
Protects me abundantly
I deserve everything, so it comes to me
I gravitate to success with the ease of each breath
She couldn't keep up
So she had to be left
Holding on to the past, almost like it suits her
She couldn't see that I was her future.
She was a cancer
She was a tumor
She would have killed me
So I had to remove her
The old me is dead and long gone
I bid her adieu
Can't remain the same, I want to be brand new
I don't feel bad that I had to off her
There was nothing more she had to offer
So, I had to upgrade,
Remain unafraid
I'm here to win so send me my accolades

About the Author

Born on July 23, 1991, Lovelee A. Lundy is the youngest of five siblings on her mother's side and the third youngest of six siblings on her father's side. Lovelee was raised in a single parent home, growing up with three out of four of her maternal siblings. Although most of her younger years were spent moving around the Midwest and East coast, she was predominantly raised in Detroit, MI from 1999-2011. After high school she enlisted in the U.S. Navy, but received honorable discharge due to unforeseen circumstances. Lovelee went on to receive her associate degree in Computer Electronic Engineering at nineteen and was hired at Intel corporation where she has built a longstanding career. Never giving up on her passion for poetry, Lovelee decided to share her passion with the world after being encouraged by her friends and family. Although Lovelee doesn't think she can change the world, she hopes to have a positive impact in it.

Connect with the Author

Instagram: Lovelee Lundy
Facebook: Lovelee Lundy
Website: http://www.LoveleeLundy.com

Lightning Source UK Ltd.
Milton Keynes UK
UKHW020639030822
406778UK00005B/78